CHIEF WOMEN
ARISE!

CHIEF WOMEN ARISE!

30 Day Women's Devotional

By
Sharon Williams
& Shana Wise

Chief Women Arise! 30 Day Women's Devotional

Copyright © 2020 Sharon Williams & Shana Wise

All rights reserved.

Dedication

To the women, past and present that have influenced my life. To the greatness, God has placed in every woman to bring glory to him. To the untapped potential of women throughout the world.

Sharon Williams

To all the King's daughters.

Shana Wise

Contents

_____

Introduction   11

            Part 1: Women of Influence   15

Chapter 1: Restored: Hannah   17

Chapter 2: A Wise Advisor: Pricilla   20

Chapter 3: An Important Dream: Pilate's Wife   23

Chapter 4: Charm Can Be Deceptive: Delilah   26

Chapter 5: Prophesy: Anna   30

Chapter 6: City Wide Influence: The Woman at the Well   33

Chapter 7: Discernment: Eve's Story   36

Chapter 8: Devotion Beyond Measure: Mary mother of Jesus   39

Chapter 9: Connection: Elizabeth   43

Chapter 10: Influence Your Community: Tabitha   46

Chapter 11: Heritage Lois: Grandmother of Timothy   49

Chapter 12: Kingdom Business Mindset: Lydia	52
Chapter 13: All In: The Widow with Two Mites	56
Chapter 14: Let's Get Our Praise On! Miriam	59
Chapter 15: Sacrifice: Jochebed, Moses' Mother	62
Chapter 16: Righteous Leadership: Deborah	65
Chapter 17: Transference: Older Women	68
Chapter 18: Share the Good News: Mary Magdalene	71
Chapter 19: Kindness: Rebekah	74
Chapter 20: Victory For the People: Jael	77
Chapter 21: Promised! The Shunammite Woman	80
Chapter 22: Who Stirs You Up?	82
Chapter 23: Precious: The Proverbs Woman	85
Chapter 24: Always Be Ready: The Bride and the Bridegroom	88
Chapter 25: Servanthood: Martha	91
Part 2: The Queens Influence	95
Chapter 26: Boldness: The Queen of Sheba	97
Chapter 27: Secure His Future: Bathsheba	99
Chapter 28: To Queen or Not: Queen Vashti	104
Chapter 29: Righteous Risk Taker: Queen Esther	110
Chapter 30: Deadly Influence: Queen Jezebel	113

Acknowledgments

To the Lord God Almighty, I am forever grateful. His presence overwhelms me every day. To the Holy Spirit my guide, who pushes me to do more than I think I can do. To Jesus Christ for saving me and giving me a purpose. To so many of you who challenged me to write.

Sharon Williams

To Jesus Christ, who is Lord of All.

Shana Wise

Introduction

"THE SPIRIT OF A CHIEF WOMEN— NOT A FEW!"

By Shana Wise

And some of them believed and consorted with Paul and Silas; and of the devout Greeks a great multitude, and of the chief women not a few. (Acts 17:4 KJV)

Therefore many of them believed; also, of honorable women which were Greeks, and of men, not a few. (Acts 17:12 KJV)

Some of the people became followers of Paul and believed. Among them was Dionysius, a member of the Areopagus, also a woman named Damaris, and a number of others. Men, not a few. (Acts 17:34 NIV)

The women in Apostle Paul's day not only believed in the Gospel of Jesus Christ, but they were also instrumental in the furtherance of the gospel in their cities, and they aided in the ministry of Paul. They were not just "regular women", they were referred to as "Chief" and "Honorable", which means that they had power and influence in their city.

We are the "chief" women of our era, even more so than the women of Paul's ministry because of the advancement in women's rights in society. We are educated, financially stable, independent, and strong together.

Women are the ones who are actively involved in the local church. We are the majority of those who attend church! Women are taking responsibilities for teaching, preaching, overseeing ministries, singing, and a host of other things to help advance the gospel of Jesus Christ.

With all this information about women and what we are doing in the church, church attendance is still on the decline. People are losing hope and faith, and many are responding to every other message except the message of Jesus Christ. There is so much hate, division, and evil going on in the world today. Chief Women are part of the solution to this problem. We have the power of the Holy Spirit residing in us and we need to activate it, in our everyday lives, to dispel the turmoil going on all around us.

Chief Women's actions are influenced by the power of the Holy Spirit. Now more than ever, chief women need to arise with the power that has been given to them and be the change in their communities. We are the ones who will aid in bringing others to Christ.

More Facts about Chief Women and Their Influence

1. Chief women use their influence to advance the Kingdom.
   - Chief women know that it is not about them, rather it is about why they were created, and how they use what God has given them to bring Him glory.
   - Chief women stand out from the crowd and others take note (vs. Acts 17:4).
   - Chief women recognize their level of authority and are good stewards of it.

2. Chief women see other women (and men) as God created them to be their sister (brother) in Christ.
   - Chief women are not intimidated, jealous, or envious by the strength and/or anointing of other women, rather they celebrate and embrace them for who they are.
   - Chief women are secure in who they are, therefore, they don't manipulate others to get what they want.
   - Chief women are always open to collaborate and work with others to enhance the body of Christ and to grow the Kingdom of God.

3. Chief women multiply (make disciples)
   - In the book of Acts, the early church grew rapidly, and many who converted were women. Women like to talk and talk about everything, but more importantly, women share information. Chief women love to share their testimonies of what God has done for them.
   - Chief women help others to walk into their destiny and purpose through discipleship.
   - Chief women are not only able to make disciples, but they can come together and make a change in various environments (home, church, and communities). Their influence is given by God, and they use it to bring others into the Kingdom and make a difference in the world.

May this book be a tool for women readers to understand the influence they have been given by God and how to use it to glorify Him within their homes, families, and communities.

Chief Women Arise!

Part One

WOMEN OF INFLUENCE

Chapter 1

RESTORED: HANNAH

By Sharon Williams

"Oh no, sir! She replied, "I haven't been drinking wine or anything stronger. But I am very discouraged, and I was pouring out my heart to the Lord. Don't think I am a wicked woman! For I have been praying out of great anguish and sorrow." "In that case, "Eli said, "go in peace! May the God of Israel grant the request you have asked of him." (1 Samuel 1:15-16 NLT)

Read 1 Samuel 1:1-28

Hannah felt inferior because she didn't have any children. She cried out to the Lord for a child. When God gave her a baby boy, she followed through with her promise to give the child to the Lord by taking him to live with the prophet. How could a mother who had so desperately wanted a child, give up her little boy to be raised by the prophet? Who does that?

Her issue wasn't about the baby, it was about her self-worth. She didn't feel complete, she felt less than those around her because in those days it was expected for every married woman to have a child. God brought her through a process of restoration by giving her what she wanted most, to be a mother. But it wasn't about having a child, it was more about being whole and accepted. She learned that God makes us whole and He accepts us. How gracious is our Lord! He taught Hannah the lesson of self-worth and gave her what she had prayed for. In return, Hannah honored God by fulfilling her promise to Him.

Questions

1. What causes you to feel inferior?

_____

_____

2. How do you deal with other people dictating who you are supposed to be?

_____

_____

3. Are you secure in your value before God?

_____

_____

Prayer

Lord God, thank you for creating me with just the right skills and tools to fulfill Your purpose. Help me, Lord, to keep Your love and acceptance as the foundation of my life. May my identity be secure in You. I am grateful to be a child of God. Amen.

Chapter 2

A WISE ADVISOR: PRICILLA

By Shana Wise

Now a certain Jew named Apollos, born at Alexandria, an eloquent man and mighty in the Scriptures, came to Ephesus. This man had been instructed in the way of the Lord; and being fervent in spirit, he spoke and taught accurately the things of the Lord, though he knew only the baptism of John. So he began to speak boldly in the synagogue. When Aquila and Priscilla heard him, they took him aside and explained to him the way of God more accurately. And when he desired to cross to Achaia, the brethren wrote, exhorting the disciples to receive him; and when he arrived, he greatly helped those who had believed through grace; for he vigorously refuted the Jews publicly, showing from the Scriptures that Jesus is the Christ. (Acts 18:24-28 NKJV)

Pricilla was a woman of wisdom, humility, and influence. She and her husband truly operated in the ministry of Christ in their marriage. They were friends and co-laborers with the Apostle Paul and they both were instrumental in sharing and spreading the gospel of Christ in their region.

On this day, Pricilla and her husband Aquila heard a man of great influence and persuasion named Apollos preaching the word of God, but he did not know that Jesus Christ had died and resurrected. They decided to speak with him afterward and explain the gospel to him. He received the word from them and started spreading the gospel of Christ immediately. Now, we do not know the exact conversation, but whatever it was, it worked! I believe that Pricilla and her husband came to Apollos with the love of Christ, and the wisdom to instruct him in a way that he was able to receive.

The lesson that we can learn from this story is that God can use your influence and knowledge of the scripture to influence other people of influence. Pricilla and Aquila recognized that Apollos loved God and he wanted others to know about him. They wanted to help him be a better preacher and evangelist by sharing the gospel with him. Their willingness to help their brother in Christ to be more effective with his passion for God is a testament to their character, integrity, and love for Jesus.

Questions

1. Have you ever been so intimidated by others' status or influence that you felt you couldn't speak with them?

   _____

   _____

2. How can you use wisdom and discernment when it comes to confronting or correcting others when they are in error or do not know the whole truth?

   _____

   _____

3. If you are married, how is God using your marriage to influence others to follow Christ?

   _____

   _____

Prayer

Father God, thank you for giving us influence with others within the ministry and in the world. Give us wisdom, understanding, humility, and discernment when it comes to correcting and confronting others who may be in error or do not know the whole truth. Show us how to operate in love and gentleness with all we encounter. Let us continue to be bold in the gospel so that it may reach others beyond our circle of influence. In Jesus' name, Amen.

Chapter 3

AN IMPORTANT DREAM: PILATE'S WIFE

By Sharon Williams

> *"Just then, as Pilate was sitting on the judgment seat, his wife sent him this message: 'Leave that innocent man alone. I suffered through a terrible nightmare about him last night."* (Matthew 27:19 NLT)

Read Matthew 27:15-26

Pontius Pilate was the fifth governor of the Roman province of Judaea, serving under Emperor Tiberius. We don't know much about Pilate's wife, but as the wife of a governor, she had a position of prominence and standing in the community. She and her husband must have had a good relationship, so much so that she was confident enough to send a message of warning to Pilate while he was sitting on the judgment seat in court. Her dream was so vivid and disturbing that she had to act on it.

God has many ways to speak to us and one of those ways is through dreams. We do not know if the wife of the governor was a believer in Jesus as the Messiah. But she understood the importance of the dream she experienced. She was compelled to respond by warning her husband.

Questions

1. Do you question the importance of your dreams?
   _____
   _____

2. When was the last time you had a dream that affected you significantly?
   _____
   _____

3. Ask God to show you what your dream means. What did He tell you about the dream?
   _____
   _____

Prayer

Father God, help me to know when you are speaking to me through my dreams. Show me what action to take from the illustration of my dreams. I desire to hear Your voice, Lord, in every way You speak to me. May I be sensitive to Your guidance when I am awake and when I am asleep. Thank you, Lord Jesus, Amen.

Chapter 4

CHARM CAN BE DECEPTIVE: DELILAH

By Shana Wise

The rulers of the Philistines went to her and said, "See if you can lure him into showing you the secret of his great strength and how we can overpower him so we may tie him up and subdue him. Each one of us will give you eleven hundred shekels of silver." (Judges 16:5 NIV)

With such nagging she prodded him day after day until he was sick to death of it. So he told her everything. "No razor has ever been used on my head," he said, "because I have been a Nazirite dedicated to God from my mother's womb. If my head were shaved, my strength would leave me, and I would become as weak as any other man." When Delilah saw that he had told her everything, she sent word to the rulers of the Philistines, "Come back once more; he has told me everything." So, the rulers of the Philistines returned with the silver in their hands. After putting him to sleep on her lap, she called for someone to shave off the seven braids of his hair, and so began to subdue him. And his strength left him. Then she called, "Samson, the Philistines are upon you!" He awoke from his sleep and thought, "I'll go out as before and shake myself free." But he did not know that the Lord had left him. (Judges 16:16-20)

Read Judges Chapter 16

This story is used to be an example to the women with the influence of knowing how to "use what they got to get what they want". Delilah had influence over a man who loved her, but she did not love him back. Delilah's deceptive actions and fake feelings towards Samson were driven by money, power, and greed. She manipulated Samson by feeding into his weakness which was sex, nagging him, and she used her charm to get the secret of his strength. Delilah used her influence for personal gain and the results of her action "brought a strong man to his knees", and ultimately his death.

Women have the choice to use their influence for good or evil. Delilah chose to use hers for monetary gain and it caused her actions to be evil (contrary to the Word of God).

1 Timothy 6:10, *For the love of money is a root of all kinds of evil. Some people, eager for money, have wandered from the faith and pierced themselves with many griefs.* If you are a woman who men find attractive for your beauty, influence, position, and charm, be careful how you use it. The question is will you recognize that God gave it to you and that you should honor Him with it, or will you take advantage of other people?

Questions

1. In the society that we live in today, do you see other women behaving like Delilah? Give examples.

   _____

   _____

2. We do not hear about what happened to Delilah after Judges chapter 16. What do you imagine her life was like after she did what she did to Samson?

   _____

   _____

3. How are you using your influence of beauty, charm, and cleverness to be a blessing to other people and to honor God?

   _____

   _____

Prayer

Father God, we are your daughters, and you expect us to represent you on earth. Let us use what you gave us to be a blessing to the Kingdom of God and the Body of Christ. We know that true beauty comes from use knowing who we are in Christ and walking in our purpose. When men find us attractive, let us recognize how to respond to them righteously and according to your Word. Help us to be good stewards of the influence you have given us. Forgive us if we have hurt anyone for personal and selfish gain. In Jesus' name, Amen.

Chapter 5

PROPHESY: ANNA

By Sharon Williams

"Anna, a prophet, was also there in the Temple. She was the daughter of Phanuel, from the tribe of Asher, and She was very old. Her husband died when they had been married only seven years. Then she lived as a widow until she was eighty-four. She never left the Temple but stayed there day and night, worshipping God with fasting and prayer." (Luke 2:36-37 NLT)

Read Luke 2:36-38

Anna is only mentioned in these three verses of the Bible, but it is a powerful testimony of her devotion to God. She never left the Temple. Prayer and fasting were her way of life. Anna prophesied over Mary and Joseph about Jesus and the redemption of Jerusalem. Her devotion to prayer and fasting caused her to be able to hear God's voice. Anna recognized the blessing and favor on Mary because she knew the redemption of Israel was promised through scripture and she practiced a lifestyle of listening to the Lord through prayer and fasting.

Like Anna, the more time we spend worshiping, fasting, and praying the more we demonstrate the presence of the Lord through our actions in our daily lives. To hear clearly what God is saying, we must spend time cultivating a listening ear. The more time with spend with the Lord, the more we act like him.

Questions

1. If your story was written in the Bible, what would it be about?

   _____

   _____

2. Is prayer and fasting a focused discipline in your life? How can you increase this discipline in your life?

   _____

   _____

3. Do you practice listening to the Lord's voice?

   _____

   _____

Prayer

Lord God, help me be an influence on those around me. I want to demonstrate my love for you, and my heart to serve you for others to see. Show me how to be more disciplined in prayer and fasting so that I can hear you. Help me speak your words to others with boldness. Through Jesus, we pray, Amen.

Chapter 6

CITY WIDE INFLUENCE: THE WOMAN AT THE WELL

By Shana Wise

And many of the Samaritans of that city believed in Him because of the word of the woman who testified, "He told me all that I ever did." So when the Samaritans had come to Him, they urged Him to stay with them; and He stayed there two days. And many more believed because of His own word. Then they said to the woman, "Now we believe, not because of what you said, for we ourselves have heard Him and we know that this is indeed the Christ, the Savior of the world." (John 4:39-42 NKJV)

Read John 4:7-42

The woman at the well had a personal experience with Jesus that transformed her life. The conversation they had about her past, her current situation, and her religion shaped the view of who He was. This woman discovered Christ, personally, at the well near her town. When she realized who He was, she could not keep it to herself, she had to go share the good news with the town's people.

She shared with them her testimony and they believed her, so much so that they wanted to meet Jesus for themselves. When they met Jesus and listened to his words, they believed him, just like the woman did.

This woman, who was looked down upon in her society because of her lifestyle, influenced others in her city to believe in Jesus Christ. God can use anyone, despite who they are and what they have done, to bring others to Christ. This woman is such an inspiration because she received Jesus for herself, and she used her testimony to bring the masses to Christ.

Questions

1. What things from your past, if any, are hindering you from sharing the Gospel with others?

_____

_____

2. What is your testimony as it relates to what Jesus has done for you? What was your first encounter with Him like?

_____

_____

3. How can you use the influence that God gave you to make a difference in your local city?

_____

_____

Prayer

Father God, we thank you for loving us despite ourselves. You know everything about us. You know our past, present, and future. We praise you because your plans for us are bigger than our current situation. You used the woman at the well to bring the town people to You, and you can use us to bring others The Good News. We will share our testimony with others because we have experienced your love personally, and we want others to experience the power of your love through your son Jesus Christ. Amen.

Chapter 7

DISCERNMENT: EVE'S STORY

By Sharon Williams

"Now the serpent was craftier than any other beast of the field that the LORD God had made. He said to the woman, "Did God actually say, 'You shall not eat of any tree in the garden'?" And the woman said to the serpent, "We may eat of the fruit of the trees in the garden, but God said, 'You shall not eat of the fruit of the tree that is in the midst of the garden, neither shall you touch it, lest you die.'" But the serpent said to the woman, "You will not surely die." (Genesis 3:1-4 ESV)

Read Genesis 3:1-20

Eve listened to the serpent and believed the lie he told her. She did not use her 'God-given' discernment to interpret the schemes of the enemy. Adam and Eve walked with God in the garden, yet Eve did not use the understanding and wisdom she had learned by being in fellowship with Almighty God. She made a choice to be persuaded to eat the forbidden fruit instead of staying true to God. Sometimes the wrong choice can be very enticing.

We can learn from Eve's mistake. When we allow emotions to dictate what we do and who we listen to, it can lead to destruction. God has given His children wisdom and discernment. We can recognize the work of the enemy even in his deceptive ways if we listen to the Spirit of God. When we pursue Him whole-heartedly, God is well able to get His message to us in a way that we will hear Him.

Questions

1. Do you remember a time in your life that you knew something or someone wasn't what they pretended to be?

   _____

   _____

2. How can you pay better attention to the discernment God has given to you?

   _____

   _____

3. We are given choices every day to do the right thing or choose to be rebellious, will you commit to doing the right thing when it is revealed to you?

_____

_____

Prayer

Almighty God, help me to pay attention to Your discernment in every situation. Give me listening ears and seeing eyes so that I can make the right decisions. Thank you, Lord Jesus, for Your help to be strong enough to make good choices. Amen.

Chapter 8

DEVOTION BEYOND MEASURE: MARY MOTHER OF JESUS

By Shana Wise

These all continued with one accord in prayer and supplication, with the women and Mary the mother of Jesus, and with His brothers. (Acts 1:14 NKJV)

I titled this Devotion Beyond Measure because when I think about the life of Mary and her continued devotion to Christ beyond his physical death and the early church, it is truly amazing!

What amazes me about Mary the mother of Jesus is her devotion to the church after her son died. Mary experienced and witnessed many things concerning Christ. From his conception within her by the Holy Spirit, rearing him as a child, seeing him minister as an adult, watching him die on the cross, and experiencing his resurrection-what a journey! After all these things she experienced physically, emotionally, and spiritually, she still chose to use her influence to help aid in the formation of the early church in Jerusalem!

I believe that Mary knew within her soul that Jesus was not her son, but God in the flesh. She was able to emotionally separate her role as earthly mother to Jesus and understand that Jesus was the Christ, the Savior of the World. Mary was a believer, witness, and disciple of Jesus Christ. The early church benefitted from her presence and devotion to the work of the ministry. Her wisdom, knowledge, and personal experience were instrumental in the development of the early church, and her witness and belief in Jesus Christ help to strengthen and shape the faith of many.

There will come a time in the lives all mothers' lives' where like Mary, we will have to separate from our children physically and emotionally. It may come through letting them go and grow as adults, our death or theirs, or just changing our role in their lives to become more of their sister in Christ rather than the role of mother. In all these instances, there will be times when it is painful, unbearable, and uncomfortable yet we must understand that it is not about us but Christ. Our children are a gift from God, and they belong to him, not us. This journey in life with our children, whether it seems good or not, is another testimony to the power of Christ within our lives. He is bringing us to a deeper devotion and trust in him through our relationship with others-including our children.

The lesson we learn from Mary is her strength to persevere and her devotion to Christ and his church despite all she had to endure. She chose to serve and use her influence to grow God's church.

Questions

1. What challenges as a mother have you had to endure with your children? How did God help you with them?

   _____

   _____

2. Are you still able to serve others despite what you may be currently going through?

   _____

   _____

3. What other attributes of Mary do you see as it relates to her role as mother and disciple of Christ?

   _____

   _____

Prayer

Father God thank you for your son, Jesus Christ. What Jesus did for us on the cross causes us to be devoted to your church and your people. Help us, women, to serve beyond our feelings and emotions. Let us remember the devotion you have towards us which is your love. Let us use the influence you gave us to inspire others to follow Christ. We dedicate our children to you. We thank you for using them to show us more of You. In Jesus' name, Amen.

Chapter 9

CONNECTION: ELIZABETH

By Sharon Williams

"And when Elizabeth heard the greeting of Mary, the baby leaped in her womb. And Elizabeth was filled with the Holy Spirit, and she exclaimed with a loud cry, "Blessed are you among women and blessed is the fruit of your womb!" (Luke 1: 41-42 ESV)

Read Luke 1:39-45

Elizabeth's sensitivity to the Lord through the baby leaping within her shows us that she was a woman listening to the Holy Spirit. She was connected to God. She knew the voice of the Lord and recognized it when He spoke to her. She cried out with boldness to Mary and confirmed that Mary's child would be blessed. Imagine what an encouragement this was to Mary as a young soon to be a mother.

Elizabeth's connection as a relative to Mary and her connection to the Lord created a strong bond of trust so when the word of the Lord came to Elizabeth it was easy for Mary to hear and receive.

When we practice listening to the Lord's voice, we can be bold to declare what God is speaking through us. There is a special faith that comes with knowing you have heard His voice. Practice staying connected with God through prayer and connected to those God has placed in the sphere of your influence.

Questions

1. Do you recognize the voice of the Lord when He speaks to you?

   _____
   _____

2. How do you practice staying connected to God daily?

   _____
   _____

3. Are you willing to cry out loud when you know others need to hear what God is saying?

   _____
   _____

Prayer

Lord, help me to be sensitive to your voice. As I listen carefully, I know you will speak in such a way that I can recognize you speaking. Give me boldness to act upon what you are saying to me. May I be an encouragement to those around me as I proclaim Your message of wisdom and grace. Amen

Chapter 10

INFLUENCE YOUR COMMUNITY: TABITHA

By Shana Wise

At Joppa there was <u>a certain disciple</u> named Tabitha, which is translated Dorcas. <u>This woman was full of good works and charitable deeds which she did.</u> But it happened in those days that she became sick and died. When they had washed her, <u>they laid her in an upper room.</u> And since Lydda was near Joppa, and the disciples had heard that Peter was there, they sent two men to him, imploring him not to delay in coming to them. Then Peter arose and went with them. When he had come, they brought him to the upper room. And all the widows stood by him weeping, showing the tunics and garments which Dorcas had made while she was with them. But Peter put them all out, and knelt down and prayed. And turning to the body he said, "Tabitha, arise." And she opened her eyes, and when she saw

Peter she sat up. Then he gave her his hand and lifted her up; and when he had called the saints and widows, <u>he presented her alive.</u> And it became known throughout all Joppa, and many believed on the Lord. So it was that he stayed many days in Joppa with Simon, a tanner. (Acts 9:36-43 NKJV)

Tabitha was a disciple of Jesus Christ. The bible also states that she was full of good works and charitable deeds. These good works were not unnoticed in the community where she lived, especially amongst the believers. Like the disciple Tabitha, we also need to be known not for our titles, or that we are a "Christian", but people should remember us by how we treat them and make them feel. If someone were to ask about your character in the community, what would be their feedback? Would they only know you for your title and position, or would they speak about your good works? Tabitha was one of the chief women in the book of Acts. She was a believer whose influence impacted those around her.

Tabitha's story shows us that just because we are believers doesn't mean that we are not going to suffer. Tabitha died, but the power of the Holy Spirit rose her back to life! The town knew her as a disciple of Christ, but now they saw her as a miracle, a living testimony to the power of God. Tabitha's influence in her community brought others to Christ.

Questions

1. Like Tabitha, you are a witness and disciple for Christ. What work does God have for you to do this year?

   _____

   _____

2. What work are you doing in your local community to serve others?

   _____

   _____

3. Has your testimony led other people to believe God?

   _____

   _____

Prayer

Father, we are your disciples, not just in name or title only but through our works. Tabitha was an example of how people should know us in our community, for our good works and deeds. Thank you for allowing us to be of service to others in our community. Thank you for using us to display your good works on the earth. In Jesus' name, Amen.

Chapter 11

HERITAGE LOIS: GRANDMOTHER OF TIMOTHY

By Sharon Williams

"I remember your genuine faith, for you share the faith that first filled your grandmother Lois and your mother, Eunice. And I know that same faith continues strong in you." (2 Timothy 1:5 NLT)

Read 2 Timothy 1:1-7

Timothy had a strong family foundation of faith. He learned from his mother and grandmother how to be faith-filled in serving God. It seems that Lois set the precedence for her family to follow the teachings of Jesus and serve the Lord. She created a legacy of service to God that was carried on through generations. We can be encouraged by the fact that one woman can make a difference in her family and influence those around her.

We also have the God-given ability to show by example how to live a Godly life not just to our families but to all those around us. People are watching to see how we consistently act like Jesus. Set precedence in your family to be an example of a household dedicated to serving the Lord. Be an influencer like Lois, Eunice, and Timothy.

Questions

1. In what ways, positive or negative, have you been influenced by family members or friends?

   _____

   _____

2. What will people say when asked how you have demonstrated a life of faith to them?

   _____

   _____

3. List three ways you can show kindness, love, and devotion to Jesus in your everyday life.

   _____

   _____

Prayer

Father God, show me how to be a godly influence on those around me. Help me lead a life of faith and dedication to You. Purify my heart, O God, so that I can be a better example of your goodness and mercy. Amen.

Chapter 12

KINGDOM BUSINESS MINDSET: LYDIA

By Shana Wise

From there we traveled to Philippi, a Roman colony and the leading city of that district of Macedonia. And we stayed there several days. On the Sabbath we went outside the city gate to the river, where we expected to find a place of prayer. We sat down and began to speak to the women who had gathered there. One of those listening was a woman from the city of Thyatira named Lydia, a dealer in purple cloth. She was a worshiper of God. The Lord opened her heart to respond to Paul's message. When she and the members of her household were baptized, she invited us to her home. "If you consider me a believer in the Lord," she said, "come and stay at my house." And she persuaded us. After Paul and Silas came out of the prison, they went to Lydia's house, where they met with the broth-

ers and sisters and encouraged them. Then they left. (Acts 16:12-15, 40 NKJV)

Lydia is a great example of how a godly businesswoman should strive to be. She did not let her business and wealth overshadow her relationship with God. Accepting Jesus Christ as her Lord and Savior gave her a new perspective and focus on her daily activities. Her life as a businesswoman blossomed into evangelism. She accepted Christ and so did her whole family. Lydia helped to establish the first church of Philippi and she aided the ministry of Paul and Silas. God used Lydia and her business for something bigger than her, the Kingdom. She chose to honor and serve God, her works lasted long after her. She left a legacy.

Questions

1. What legacy are you working towards through the business/ministry God has given you?

   _____

   _____

2. Your business is a tool given to you to grow the Kingdom of God. We must grow from seeing "a customer" to seeing "an opportunity" to witness for Christ. How comfortable are you with ministering and

witnessing to others? Any hindrances?

_____

_____

3. As believers in the body of Christ, we should never go into business to make money, rather, we should approach business as an opportunity to use the resources that God blesses us with to expand our territory and influence for the Kingdom's sake. What are your business goals for this year, and how do they connect with your Kingdom purpose?

_____

_____

4. Many of us use the social network to meet others and grow our business. I always pray to the Lord about where I should go and who I should connect with-I call them Kingdom connections. These types of relationships mirror the principles of giving and receiving, sowing, and reaping. Reflect on the Kingdom connections you have made so far. What is your and/or their purpose in your life other than business?

_____

_____

5. Lydia was a seller of purple and purple cloth symbolizes royalty. Lydia probably sold to people in high places which is an area of influence. How are you using the influence that God gave you?

_____

_____

Prayer

Father God, thank you for trusting me with the business and/or ministry that you have for me to oversee. Help me to see opportunities to witness to everyone I encounter within the marketplace. Give me wisdom and insight through your Holy Spirit to be your witness in the world system marketplace. Like Lydia, let me be the woman to influence my home, community, and marketplace for your glory. In Jesus' name, Amen.

Chapter 13

ALL IN: THE WIDOW WITH TWO MITES

By Sharon Williams

"For they all contributed out of their abundance, but she out of her poverty put in all she had to live on." (Luke 21:4 ESV)

Read Luke 21:1-4

Out of her lack, this widow gave all she had. Many of us struggle just to give 10% in a tithe to the church. Many think they cannot afford to tithe because money is so tight and there are bills to be paid. But the Bible teaches us that we cannot afford not to tithe because there is a blessing poured out on us when we are generous with our giving to the Lord. This widow understood that everything she had was given to her by God and all that she had was only because of God's gift to her, therefore, everything belonged to Him. There is a special blessing that comes when we give more than is required. There is freedom in giving generously that keeps us from holding on too tightly to what we have.

Jesus also was calling attention to the fact that the people in the synagogue were not taking care of this widow as they had been told to do. All she had left was 2 mites. She was demonstrating to everyone that she was left with nothing. Deuteronomy 14:28-29, states there is a blessing when we take care of orphans and widows. Deuteronomy 27:19 says cursed is anyone who denies justice to foreigners, orphans, or widows (NLT).

Questions

1. Do you hold back from being generous? Are you willing to give generously when prompted by the Lord?

    _____

    _____

2. Do you trust God completely to take care of your needs?

    _____

    _____

3. Will you commit to helping orphans, widows, and foreigners?

_____

_____

Prayer

Lord Jesus, I repent for those times I haven't been generous. I acknowledge that You have given me everything I have, it all belongs to You. Help me, Lord, to hold onto all that you have given me with open hands and an open heart to give generously. In the name of Jesus, Amen.

Chapter 14

LET'S GET OUR PRAISE ON! MIRIAM

By Shana Wise

> *Then Miriam the prophetess, the sister of Aaron, took the timbrel in her hand; and all the women went out after her with timbrels and with dances. And Miriam answered them: "Sing to the Lord, For He has triumphed gloriously! The horse and its rider He has thrown into the sea!"* (Exodus 15:20-21 NKJV)

Miriam: Moses and Aaron's sister led all the women that had just been freed from Egypt into praise and worship. She used her influence not only to praise God for herself but to lead others to join in. Miriam witnessed God move on behalf of the Israelites in the land of Egypt through her brother Moses who set them free from the bondage of slavery.

The Israelites crossed the Red Sea on dry land, and she witnessed it with her own eyes Pharaoh and his army were defeated by the hand of God. Miriam could have chosen to do anything, but she chose to use her influence and leadership as a prophetess to have the women engage in singing, dancing, and playing timbrels, unto the Lord their God.

Let us remember no matter what is going on in our lives, God will always show up on our behalf, because he loves us. When he delivers us, we owe Him praise of thanksgiving and adoration!

Questions

1. When were the last time you praised God for what he did for you, your family, and other people?

　_____

　_____

2. Have you ever been in bondage and set free? What was that feeling like? How did God deliver you?

　_____

　_____

3. How are you using your influence within your community to engage them in worshipping God?

　_____

　_____

4. If you have a leadership role within your church, how are you using your gifts to empower others?

_____

_____

Prayer

Father God, we thank you for delivering us from the hand of the enemy. We have seen you show up for us repeatedly when our backs were against the wall and there was no way out. You showed up on our behalf because you love us. We praise you with all our being because of who You are in our lives. You have been better than good to us, and we say thank you. In Jesus' name, Amen.

Chapter 15

SACRIFICE: JOCHEBED, MOSES' MOTHER

By Sharon Williams

> *"By faith Moses, when he was born, was hidden for three months by his parents, because they saw that the child was beautiful, and they were not afraid of the king's edict."* (Hebrews 11:23 ESV)

Read Exodus 2:1-10

> *"The name of Amram's wife was Jochebed the daughter of Levi, who was born to Levi in Egypt. And she bore to Amram; Aaron and Moses and Miriam their sister."* (Numbers 26:59 ESV)

Jochebed saved the life of her child by hiding him in the Nile River. It was in this same river that Pharaoh declared every Hebrew male child should be drowned. What great faith and sacrifice this mother had to release her son into the river in a basket, placing his fate in the hands of God. Of course, it was the same river where so much death was taking place! God takes the dark things of this world and turns them around for good. His purposes will prevail.

God shows His mercy by giving baby Moses back to his mother to care for in the first months of his life. Jochebed followed through with her promise after baby Moses was weaned, she took her son back to Pharaoh's daughter to raise as her son. Imagine if Jochebed had decided to run away with her children and try to escape with her family. God's purposes are not always clear to us. Sometimes we want to run away and hide because we don't understand or trust the outcome. But trusting the Lord completely brings supernatural results.

Questions

1. How much are you willing to give up for God's purpose in your life and the lives of your loved ones?

___

___

2. Do you completely trust God with every person, every possession, every talent you have, or do you hold on too tightly to some?

___

___

3. Jochebed disobeyed the edict of the king to save her child. When is it right or wrong to disobey the laws of the land?

_____

_____

Prayer

Lord Jesus, help me make wise choices with your guidance and help along the way. May I trust you completely with every relationship, every talent, and every pursuit. Help me, Lord God, to do all for Your glory. In the name of Jesus, Amen.

Chapter 16

RIGHTEOUS LEADERSHIP: DEBORAH

By Shana Wise

> *Now Deborah, a prophetess, the wife of Lapidoth, was judging Israel at that time. And she would sit under the palm tree of Deborah between Ramah and Bethel in the mountains of Ephraim. And the children of Israel came up to her for judgment.* (Judges 4:4-5 NKJV)

Read Judges chapters 4-5

Many know the judge Deborah as the one who went with Barak into battle, or how she sang songs of praise unto God after the battle when Israel won the victory, but before all these happenings, she was a prophetess and wife that sat under a palm tree and gave judgment.

The children of Israel looked to Deborah as their spiritual leader, a woman of wisdom, and one who lead them to worship God. She used her God-given influence on a national level from the office of her palm tree.

Deborah judged the children of Israel righteously. She was anointed by God to carry this title and position worthily. The children of Israel had respect for her so much, that Barak, the leader of the army, wanted her to come with him to fight the enemy. Deborah did not fight in the battle, but her presence gave the army courage to overcome the enemy.

The bible doesn't mention Deborah as the mother to biological children, but the children of Israel regarded her as their spiritual mother and righteous judge.

Questions

1. Who has been a mother figure to you? Are you a mother figure to anyone?

_____

_____

2. Deborah had national influence. What do you think this world would be like if we had more leaders that lead righteously?

_____

_____

3. Deborah was multi-gifted in her anointing. What gifts has God given you and how are you using them?

_____

_____

Prayer

Father God, thank you for all the mother and father figures in our life. We thank you that their righteous style of living inspired us to want to live right and worship You. Help us to judge and/or discern righteously amongst your people. Let us be the role models of the Kingdom, just like Deborah. In Jesus' name, Amen.

Chapter 17

TRANSFERENCE: OLDER WOMEN

By Sharon Williams

> *"Teach the older women to live in a way that honors God. They must not slander others or be heavy drinkers. Instead, they should teach others what is good. These older women must train the younger women to love their husbands and their children, to live wisely and be pure, to care for their homes, to do good, and to be submissive to their husbands. Then they will not bring shame on the word of God."* (Titus 2:3-5 NLT)

Read Titus 2:1-11

The term older women in this text do not necessarily mean older in age, but a better definition would be mature women. Each of us is mature in comparison to someone else with less experience. We should all have someone in our lives that we can learn from and someone that can learn from us. The

African proverb says, 'he/she who runs alone thinks he/she runs fastest.' We need trusted mentors to show us areas we need to improve. Sometimes we may need to hear that we are doing well and making progress.

You may think you have nothing to teach to younger women but as you go over the list from these verses, you see that most characteristics in this list talk about everyday life. How to be a good wife, living wisely, how to be pure, how to serve God, and how to love one another. Each of us has areas of growth that we can share with someone else.

Questions

1. How can you learn from the women around you?

   _____

   _____

2. What skills do you have that you can share?

   _____

   _____

3. How can you be more open to what others can teach you?

   _____

   _____

Prayer

Lord, make me more pliable in Your hands. I desire to learn from You and those around me. Help me to be aware and open to grow and develop as a mature woman of God. Help me be a good example to young women and look for ways to be an encouragement. In Jesus' name, Amen.

Chapter 18

SHARE THE GOOD NEWS: MARY MAGDALENE

By Shana Wise

Mary Magdalene came and told the disciples that she had seen the Lord, and that He had spoken these things to her. (John 20:18 NKJV)

Read John 20:1-18

Mary Magdalene was the first one to see Jesus risen from the dead at his tomb. She was a follower of Christ before his death. She witnessed him die on the cross, and she helped prepare his body for his burial. She also was the one who checked on his body in the tomb. What a committed woman to Christ!

Mary and Christ had a conversation at the tomb, and he stated: John 20:17, *Jesus said to her, "Do not cling to Me, for I have not yet ascended to My Father; but go to My brethren and say to them, 'I am ascending to My Father and your Father, and to My God and your God.'"*. Mary immediately went to find the disciples and shared the news about Christ's resurrection.

Mary's commitment to Christ caused her to follow him and believe in His words. It made her be compelled to obey him by sharing the news with the other disciples. Mary used her influence as a follower of Christ to share the news that He Has Risen. What an awesome message to deliver, especially to those of the faith, and the ones who have yet to believe!

Questions

1. How have you experienced the resurrection of Christ in your life?

   _____

   _____

2. How do you use your influence as a follower of Christ to witness to the lost?

   _____

   _____

3. Mary Magdalene was committed to Christ and his words. In what areas of your life can you be more committed to Him?

   _____

   _____

Prayer

Jesus, we praise your name because you have risen. We have all been "at the empty tombs" of life, but we are grateful that you are there: alive and risen. We thank you for the eternal life that we have through your death, burial, and resurrection. Due to this fact, we are committed to sharing the Good News with all those you have placed in our lives. In Jesus' Name, Amen.

Chapter 19

KINDNESS: REBEKAH

By Sharon Williams

> *"After she had given him a drink, she said, "I'll draw water for your camels too, until they have had enough to drink." So she quickly emptied her jar into the trough, ran back to the well to draw more water, and drew enough for all his camels."* (Genesis 24:19-20 NLT)

Read Genesis 24:1-67

> *"Then they said, "Let's call the young woman and ask her about it." So they called Rebekah and asked her, "Will you go with this man?" "I will go," she said.* (Genesis 24:57-58 NLT)

Rebekah was willing to help strangers when they had a need. Before she knew who these men were, she served not only them but also their camels. When she became Isaac's wife these same camels belonged to her husband. She was taking care of her future before she knew what her future was to be. God prepares us before He calls us. He goes before us and prepares the way.

She was willing to go with these men without delay, she saw her destiny and embraced it whole-heartedly without fear. She left her family and her home to go to a foreign land and marry a man she had never met. Rebekah was trusting in God and her family's decisions for her future. Rebekah walked in obedience and was rewarded and honored because of it.

Questions

1. Are you willing to respond when you see a need, even for strangers?

   _____
   _____

2. Do you trust God completely with your future?

   _____
   _____

3. Are there times in your past when God showed up unexpectedly and did amazing things for you?

   _____
   _____

Prayer

Lord, help me see the needs around me and respond as you guide me. I trust you with my life and my future, help me with my moments of doubt. You, Lord God, are more than enough for every situation in my life and I acknowledge your guiding hand leading me every step of the way. In the name of Your Son, Jesus Christ our Lord, Amen.

Chapter 20

VICTORY FOR THE PEOPLE: JAEL

By Shana Wise

Sisera, meanwhile, fled on foot to the tent of Jael, the wife of Heber the Kenite, because there was an alliance between Jabin king of Hazor and the family of Heber the Kenite Jael went out to meet Sisera and said to him, "Come, my lord, come right in. Don't be afraid." So he entered her tent, and she covered him with a blanket. "I'm thirsty," he said. "Please give me some water." She opened a skin of milk, gave him a drink, and covered him up. "Stand in the doorway of the tent," he told her. "If someone comes by and asks you, 'Is anyone in there?' say 'No.'" But Jael, Heber's wife, picked up a tent peg and a hammer and went quietly to him while he lay fast asleep, exhausted. She drove the peg through his temple into the ground, and he died. Just then Barak came by in pursuit of Sisera, and Jael went out to

> *meet him. "Come," she said, "I will show you the man you're looking for." So he went in with her, and there lay Sisera with the tent peg through his temple – dead. On that day God subdued Jabin king of Canaan before the Israelites.* (Judges 4:17-23 NIV)

Jael was cunning with the way she executed her enemy. Sisera thought he was safe and could hide in the tent of Jael, little did he know that she was not afraid to kill the enemy that had been suppressing her people for years.

Jael is an example of a different way to fight. She engaged her enemy with a tactic that caught her enemy off guard. She ambushed him! She played off his weakness <u>of thinking he was safe because he was in the presence of a woman.</u>

She used her influence of being a woman and her influence of courage when it came to killing Sisera without hesitation. She knew who the enemy was, and she killed him in her house (tent). This was a victory for only not Jael, but all of Israel.

Questions

1. Have you ever been in a situation where you were underestimated by someone else because you were a woman?

_____

_____

2. Have you ever had "the enemy (spirit, situation, or circumstance)" enter your home and you had to rid it from your house?

   _____

   _____

3. Jael's "no fear" attitude and willingness to kill the enemy who had been suppressing her people caused victory for other people. What lesson can you learn from this story that would help you use your influence to help someone else?

   _____

   _____

Prayer

Father, help us to have bold faith like Jael when confronting the enemy. Remind us that you have given us power and authority over our adversaries. Let us use the influence you gave us as women to be used in a way that brings you glory and benefits others for the good. Forgive us for any tolerance of compromise in our homes. Holy Spirit, show us how to overcome any fear in our lives. In Jesus' name, Amen.

Chapter 21

PROMISED! THE SHUNAMMITE WOMAN

By Sharon Williams

"As she approached the man of God at Mount Carmel, Elisha saw her in the distance. He said to Gehazi, 'Look the woman from Shunem is coming. Run out to meet her and ask her, 'Is everything all right with you, your husband and your child?' "Yes, the woman told Gehazi, "everything is fine." (2 Kings 4:25-26 NLT)

Read 2 Kings 4:8-37

This woman from Shunem had a promise given to her that she would have a son.

When it seemed that the promise failed, she went to the source of the promise. (Her source was the prophet of God, our source is now Jesus) She was so confident of the promise that she could, with all sincerity say, 'everything is fine,' even when her son was dying.

There was no 'plan B' in her mind and no doubt, only the source of the promise had the answer, not the servant, not a doctor, no one else, only the man of God. She did not question or second guess what God had said through the prophet. She held firmly to the promise.

Questions

1. What gave her the aggressive pursuit to contend for her son?

   _____

   _____

2. What can we learn from the Shunammite woman?

   _____

   _____

3. What promise from God are you holding on to?

   _____

   _____

Prayer

Lord God, help me to have the confidence in Your promises to trust You with the answers. I trust in Your timing, Lord, and believe that You will fulfill Your Word. Help me to focus on You as I wait. Thank you for provision and eyes to see as You see. In Jesus' name, Amen.

Chapter 22

WHO STIRS YOU UP?

By Shana Wise

> *And the word of the Lord was being spread throughout all the region. But the Jews stirred up the devout and prominent women and the chief men of the city, raised up persecution against Paul and Barnabas, and expelled them from their region.* (Acts 13:49-50 NKJV)

Read Acts 13:14-52

Paul and Barnabas were on a missionary trip in Antioch preaching the gospel to the Gentiles and Jews. Many people in the city believed and converted to Christianity. This made the prominent Jewish leaders in the region who did not believe to be filled with jealousy and envy. They opposed Paul and Barnabas by speaking against their teaching and stirring up discontent against them through the men and women that influenced the city. Paul and Barnabas were expelled from the region due to the stirring up of influential people.

Women who have power, authority, and influence within their city must be careful of the motives of other people. People will use your influence for their agendas. If women don't know their purpose, they can be swayed by others to do bad things to other people. Just like the Jewish leaders used these women to persecute Paul and Barnabas for sharing the gospel, people can use women of influence to harm others. The main reason why these women were able to be used was that they didn't worship God for themselves. People had more power to stir them up than God.

Questions

1. How can we as women guard our influence against being used by others?

_____

_____

2. Have you ever used your influence in the wrong way, and it hurt other people? How have you used your influence to help other people?

_____

_____

3. What are some things that get you "stirred up" whether it is good or bad? What has been your response? What were the results?

_____

_____

Prayer

Father thank you for giving us influence in our communities. Help us to be good stewards of what you have given us. We confess those things that get us stirred up that are contrary to your Word. Forgive us for anyone that we have hurt through wrongly misusing our influence. Lead and guide us on this journey of life to be the light in our communities that you have called us to be. In Jesus' name, Amen.

Chapter 23

PRECIOUS: THE PROVERBS WOMAN

By Sharon Williams

"An excellent wife who can find. She is far more precious than jewels." (Proverbs 31:10 ESV)

Read Proverbs 31:10-31

The Proverbs woman is incredible. Who could ever measure up to the description found in these verses? When we use this portion of Scripture as a guideline for improving our character, instead of comparing our progress with her, we will achieve steps toward maturity. There are many good tips for success in these verses.

"She rises before dawn and organizes her day." (Proverbs 31:15 MSG)

> *"She is quick to assist anyone in need, reaches out to help the poor."* (Proverbs 31:20 MSG)

> *"A good woman is hard to find and worth far more than diamonds."* (Proverbs 31:10 MSG)

Like diamonds, there is a process that must be worked out in each of us. A diamond starts as a rock and requires a process to be revealed as something valuable. The diamond was valuable before the refining process. Women are precious, valuable even when we are unrefined and incomplete. We don't have to wait until we are perfect to be precious. When we work towards making progress with good character traits, we will gain the wisdom and the discipline to be a woman of excellence. We must set reasonable goals and through our endeavors; Jesus gives us help along the way.

Questions

1. Which verse from this text are you applying to your life now?

   _____

   _____

2. Do you depend on God's help to improve your character, or do you strive to do it yourself?

_____

_____

3. Do you see yourself as precious and valuable like a diamond?

_____

_____

Prayer

Lord God help me to embrace Your help as I work towards being more organized, more kind to others and improve character. Thank you that you are well pleased with my progress. I am precious to You, and You love me with an everlasting love even with my flaws. Thank you, Lord. Amen.

Chapter 24

ALWAYS BE READY: THE BRIDE AND THE BRIDEGROOM

By Sharon Williams

> *"Then the kingdom of heaven will be like ten virgins who took their lamps and went to meet the bridegroom."* (Matthew 25:1 ESV)

> *"Watch, therefore, for you know neither the day nor the hour."* (Matthew 25:13 ESV)

Read Matthew 25:1-13

The parable of the ten virgins is told by Jesus to help the disciples, and us, understand the mysteries of the Bible. In this story, five virgins waiting for the bridegroom were prepared with extra oil for their lamps. The other five virgins were not prepared with extra oil. The lesson from this parable is for us to always be prepared and watch for the Bridegroom, Jesus to come to collect His bride (the Church) for the marriage supper of the Lamb.

None of us wants to be busy and preoccupied to the point of missing Jesus when He returns. We must stay focused on His return and focused on our preparation for the moment when we see Him. We are the Bride of Christ; Jesus our Lord gave up His life on the cross so that we could be called His very own. Live each day as if Jesus is returning today. Stay aware of His presence and pray continuously.

Questions

1. Are you prepared and ready for Christ's return?

   _____
   _____

2. Are you focused on Heavenly things or things of the earth?

   _____
   _____

3. What can you do to be better prepared for the bridegroom's arrival?

   _____
   _____

Prayer

Lord Jesus, thank you for making a way for me to join you as a part of the Bride of Christ. Help me to be ready and watching for Your return. My greatest desire is to hear you, Lord God, say 'well done good and faithful servant'. In Your Holy Name, we ask, Amen.

Chapter 25

SERVANTHOOD: MARTHA

By Sharon Williams

"Now as they went on their way, Jesus entered a village. And a woman named Martha welcomed Him (Jesus) into her house." (Luke 10:38 ESV)

Read Luke 10:38-42

Most teachers focus on Martha's sister Mary because Mary chose the better part, to sit at the feet of Jesus and listen to His words. But Martha is the one who invited Jesus into their home. She welcomed Jesus and his group of followers and provided for their needs. Martha served them with a willing heart.

Her motives were pure when she invited Jesus into her house. She used her talents to minister to him and his followers. When she stopped focusing on blessing others and began to observe her sister sitting at the Lord's feet, Martha's heart changed to one of frustration and comparison. It became all about her. When we lose our focus and compare ourselves with those around us, we become selfish; we become defensive, and justify our position. When we stay within our strengths and keep our eyes on Jesus, we are content to complete our purpose and stay within our God-given abilities. God is our Defender; He will come to our rescue and provide all we need to accomplish His purpose for us.

Questions

1. What motives drive your work?

   _____

   _____

2. Who do you compete with for recognition?

   _____

   _____

3. When you feel overwhelmed and tired, what fuels you to finish?

   _____

   _____

Prayer

Lord Jesus, thank you for always coming to my rescue when I need your help. Give me the strength to finish well in every venture. Holy Spirit, be with me, guide me, and strengthen me so that God's purpose in my life is fulfilled. Amen.

Part Two

THE QUEENS INFLUENCE

Chapter 26

BOLDNESS: THE QUEEN OF SHEBA

By Sharon Williams

"When the Queen of Sheba heard of Solomon's fame, she came to Jerusalem to test him with hard questions. She arrived with a large group of attendants and a great caravan of camels loaded with spices, large quantities of gold, and precious jewels. When she met with Solomon, she talked with him about everything she had on her mind." (2 Chronicles 9:1-2 NLV)

Read 2 Chronicles 9:1-12

The Queen of Sheba came to find out if the rumors she had heard were true. She wasn't afraid to ask King Solomon hard questions. She was on that mission to discover the truth. The Queen of Sheba came to Jerusalem prepared. She brought the appropriate gifts to show her respect to the office of this mighty king. She came with a well-thought-out plan.

This queen understood her position and her authority so she could walk into King Solomon's presence with confidence and boldness. She had a purpose and a plan to fulfill it. She was seeking answers and confirmation for what she had heard. Instead of believing the stories told by others, this queen went to the one person with the answers.

Questions

1. Are you careful to show respect to those in authority?

   _____

   _____

2. Do you prepare before you go?

   _____

   _____

3. Are you willing to ask hard questions to discover the truth?

   _____

   _____

Prayer

Lord, help me to be prepared in every situation. I want to be ready to answer difficult questions when asked. Help me to be secure and bold enough to ask hard questions when necessary. Show me when the truth is being spoken and when it is not. Thank you, Lord Jesus, for Your guidance, Your grace, and Your mercy towards me. In the name of Jesus. Amen.

Chapter 27

SECURE HIS FUTURE: BATHSHEBA

By Shana Wise

And Bathsheba bowed and did homage to the king. Then the king said, "What is your wish?" Then she said to him, "My lord, you swore by the Lord your God to your maidservant, saying, 'Assuredly Solomon your son shall reign after me, and he shall sit on my throne.' So now, look! Adonijah has become king; and now, my lord the king, you do not know about it. He has sacrificed oxen and fattened cattle and sheep in abundance, and has invited all the sons of the king, Abiathar the priest, and Joab the commander of the army; but Solomon your servant he has not invited. And as for you, my lord, O king, the eyes of all Israel are on you, that you should tell them who will sit on the throne of my lord the king after him. Otherwise it will happen, when my lord the king rests with his fathers, that I and my son Solomon will be counted as offenders." And just then, while she was still talking with the king, Nathan the prophet also came in. So they told the king, saying, "Here is Nathan the prophet." And when he came in before the king, he bowed down before the king with his face to the ground. And Nathan said, "My lord, O king, have you said, 'Adonijah shall reign after me, and he shall sit on my throne'? For he has gone down today, and has sacrificed oxen and fattened cattle and sheep in abundance, and has invited all the king's sons, and the commanders of the army, and Abiathar the priest; and look! They are eating and drinking before him; and they say, 'Long live King Adonijah!' But he has not invited me — me your servant — nor Zadok the priest, nor Benaiah the son of Jehoiada, nor your servant Solomon. Has this thing been done by my lord the king, and you have not told your servant who should sit on the throne of my lord the king after him?" Then King David answered and said, "Call Bathsheba to me." So she came into the king's presence and stood before the king. And the king took an oath and said, "As the Lord lives, who has redeemed my life from every distress, just as I swore to you by the Lord God of Israel, saying, 'Assuredly Solomon your son shall be king after me, and he shall sit on my throne in my place,' so I certainly will do this day." Then Bathsheba bowed with her face to the earth, and paid homage to the king, and said, "Let my lord King David live forever!" (1 Kings 1:16-31 NKJV)

Bathsheba was the mother of Solomon, the son she had with King David. He had promised her that Solomon would succeed him as king and heir to the throne. It was towards the end of King David's life that one of his other sons, Adonijah, (not by Bathsheba) declared himself king behind his father's back. When Bathsheba heard of this unauthorized declaration by Adonijah, she went to King David and told him what was happening and reminded him of his promise to make Solomon successor to the throne. In doing so, King David declared Solomon as king and thwarted the plans of Adonijah.

Bathsheba used the influence she had with King David to secure her son's future and promise. She knew that if she did not act immediately, her son not only could lose what was promised to him, but he could potentially lose his life because his brother Adonijah would have seen him as a threat to his unauthorized position. Solomon was young and inexperienced during this time and his mother had to take authority over the situation on his behalf.

King David responded to her plea for their son by taking immediate action and declaring him successor to the throne. He was the only one who had total authority to change the situation for Solomon, and Bathsheba knew this. In this life, especially as mothers, when we must fight for our children's future through prayer, intercession, and action. As believers, we must know where to go to change situations that may seem impossible to us, and that place is in God. Bathsheba reminded King David of his promise, and likewise, we must remind God of his promises through His Word concerning our children. King David had earthly authority as king, but we serve a God who has authority overall.

Questions

1. How has God answered your prayers of intercession concerning your children?

   _____

   _____

2. How are you using your influence as a mother to secure your children's future?

   _____

   _____

3. What promises has God made to you that have not come to pass yet concerning your loved ones? What are you believing Him for according to scripture?

   _____

   _____

Prayer

Father God, we thank you for your promises concerning us and our children. You are faithful to Your Word, and we thank you. Give us wisdom and strength to fight in faith for our children. Help us to lean and depend on you through whatever is going on and to act when it is appropriate. Thank you for the children that you have assigned to us and continue to lead us in how to raise them in You. In Jesus' name, Amen.

Chapter 28

TO QUEEN OR NOT: QUEEN VASHTI

By Shana Wise

In accordance with the law, the drinking was not compulsory; for so the king had ordered all the officers of his household, that they should do according to each man's pleasure. Queen Vashti also made a feast for the women in the royal palace which belonged to King Ahasuerus. On the seventh day, when the heart of the king was merry with wine, he commanded Mehuman, Biztha, Harbona, Bigtha, Abagtha, Zethar, and Carcas, seven eunuchs who served in the presence of King Ahasuerus, to bring Queen Vashti before the king, wearing her royal crown, in order to show her beauty to the people and the officials, for she was beautiful to behold. But Queen Vashti refused to come at the king's command brought by his eunuchs; therefore the king was furious, and his anger burned within him. Then the king said to the wise men who understood the times (for this was the king's manner toward all who knew law and justice, those closest to him being Carshena, Shethar, Admatha, Tarshish, Meres, Marsena, and Memucan, the seven princes of Persia and Media, who had access to the king's presence, and who ranked highest in the kingdom): "What shall we do to Queen Vashti, according to law, because she did not obey the command of King Ahasuerus brought to her by the eunuchs?" And Memucan answered before the king and the princes: "Queen Vashti has not only wronged the king, but also all the princes, and all the people who are in all the provinces of King Ahasuerus. For the queen's behavior will become known to all women, so that they will despise their husbands in their eyes, when they report, 'King Ahasuerus commanded Queen Vashti to be brought in before him, but she did not come.' This very day the noble ladies of Persia and Media will say to all the king's officials that they have heard of the behavior of the queen. Thus there will be excessive contempt and wrath. If it pleases the king, let a royal decree go out from him, and let it be recorded in the laws of the Persians and the Medes, so that it will not be altered, that Vashti shall come no more before King Ahasuerus; and let the king give her royal position to

> *another who is better than she. When the king's decree which he will make is proclaimed throughout all his empire (for it is great), all wives will honor their husbands, both great and small." And the reply pleased the king and the princes, and the king did according to the word of Memucan. Then he sent letters to all the king's provinces, to each province in its own script, and to every people in their own language, that each man should be master in his own house and speak in the language of his own people.*
> (Esther 1:8-22 NKJV)

The story of Queen Vashti is very interesting because the way she chose to use her influence in the kingdom had various consequences that affected her queenship and it changed the law of the land which directly affected the people of the land.

Queen Vashti refused to come to King Ahasuerus's party because he and all the men in the room had been drinking for seven days. The king wanted Vashti to come and parade in front of him at his party. Many commentaries suggest the king wanted Vashti to parade naked, or that she may have been pregnant, and/or it was not the custom for Persian women to appear before a public gathering of men. For whatever reason, Queen Vashti refused to obey the king's request. This made the king mad, and he decided, under the influence of alcohol, to banish Queen Vashti from the land, and institute a law in the land concerning husbands and their wives. The king gave the men in the land a stronger hold on their wives so that they would not follow the pattern of Queen Vashti.

We never heard about Queen Vashti again, but we do know that her decision had consequences that affected everyone in the kingdom. The way she chose to use her influence can be viewed as good or bad depending on how you interpret her actions. She chose not to compromise her worth as a woman during a time when that was unheard of. Women, in biblical times, did not have any or very limited rights. Their value was a little above a dog-even if they had the title of a queen. The queen was probably protecting her dignity because if she entered a room with many drunken men, who knew what would have happened to her. She could have been raped by multiple men or made to perform sexual acts with her husband in front of them, and/or she could have been touched and mishandled inappropriately. If she was pregnant, this would have been very devastating to her and her unborn child.

On the other hand, her refusal to come to the king made him feel less than a man. The king chose to listen to his advisors, while he was intoxicated and mad, to decide about Queen Vashti and to change the law in the land so that her influence would not carry over to the other women of the land. Also, her refusing to come to him, and the king not addressing her actions, could have led Queen Vashti to feel like she could continue to challenge the king's authority.

Either way, Queen Vashti chose to use her influence to think about herself and her wellbeing despite the consequences for her and the other women in the kingdom. Yet, despite all this, Queen Vashti's removal paved the way for another queen, Esther, to come and save the lives of the Jews in the land.

Questions

1. There will be times, as a woman, when we must choose whether to compromise or not, our values at a request of a man (or woman). Have you ever had to make this choice? What were the results?

   _____

   _____

2. Queen Vashti used her influence to look out for her wellbeing, despite the consequences. Have you ever had to do that? What were the results?

   _____

   _____

3. Many women are in oppressing relationships. How can we help them in a way that pleases God?

_____

_____

Prayer

Father, we thank you for loving us as your daughters. In You, we find out who we are and the plans and purpose for our life. Help us to use our influence to be a blessing to others and ourselves. Let us as women, help other women to "adjust their crown" by loving, uplifting, and encouraging one another. In Jesus' name, amen.

Chapter 29

RIGHTEOUS RISK TAKER: QUEEN ESTHER

By Shana Wise

"Go, gather all the Jews who are present in Shushan, and fast for me; neither eat nor drink for three days, night or day. My maids and I will fast likewise. And so I will go to the king, which is against the law; and if I perish, I perish!" (Esther 4:16 NKJV)

Read the entire book of Esther

Many of us have taken risks that could have cost us everything, including our very own lives, but was it a righteous decision? Most of the time, we take a risk-based on flesh and feelings, not considering the consequences of our actions. Queen Esther, however, used her influence with her husband, King Ahasuerus, to save her people. By doing this, she risked her life because he did not know that she was an

Israelite, and she was not allowed by law to go to him without being summoned.

There was a plot by a man named Haman, one of the kings' officials, to kill all the Jews in the land. When Queen Esther got word of this, she told her people to fast for her because she was about to risk her life to save them. What a brave and unselfish woman to use her influence in that way! Because she was brave and took a righteous risk, she ended up saving her people from the plot of the enemy!

Questions

1. When was the last time you took a risk? Did you fast and pray before you did it? What were the results?

   _____

   _____

2. Queen Esther was a beautiful woman, therefore the king married her. Yet, she did not use her beauty for selfish gain, she used her influence to save her people. How are others benefiting from your beautiful influence in the land?

   _____

   _____

3. Christ gave his life so that we may have eternal life. In what ways can you be more intentional about bringing life to someone else?

_____

_____

Prayer

Father God, we thank you for showing us how to be righteous risk-takers. You have given us influence in the land to show off your glory. Continue to show us how to be a blessing to others. Let us have the unselfish spirit like Queen Esther. Let us use our beautiful influence to bring life to others through your son Jesus Christ. Amen

Chapter 30

DEADLY INFLUENCE: QUEEN JEZEBEL

By Shana Wise

For so it was, while Jezebel massacred the prophets of the Lord, that Obadiah had taken one hundred prophets and hidden them, fifty to a cave, and had fed them with bread and water.) (1 Kings 18:4 NKJV)

Then Jezebel sent a messenger to Elijah, saying, "So let the gods do to me, and more also, if I do not make your life as the life of one of them by tomorrow about this time." (1 Kings 19:2)

Read 1 Kings 21:7-15: The story of Naboth (an innocent man) put to death because of Jezebel's manipulation.

Queen Jezebel was one of the evilest queens that lived in biblical times. She used her influence to make murderous threats and kill the innocent. She used her influence to manipulate her husband King Ahab into acts of ungodliness.

Jezebel was a worshipper of Baal, and she influenced her husband and the nation of Israel to worship Baal. This was a great evil in the eyes of God because his children were only supposed to worship the true and living God.

Elijah, God's true prophet at the time, would give messages from God to King Ahab regarding his disobedience, sin, and evil ways. King Ahab did not like this, nor did his wife Jezebel. Jezebel hated not only Elijah, but she also hated righteousness and truth. She had the prophets of God murdered because she wanted her prophets of Baal to influence the land. Jezebel wanted to kill Elijah after he called down fire from heaven (by God) at Mt. Carmel. Elijah's demonstration of the power of God over Baal, at the altar of Mt. Carmel, influenced the people to fear and turn back to God and they helped him kill all of Jezebel's false prophets at the altar (read 1 Kings chapters 18 and 19).

Jezebel plotted to have Naboth killed because he would not sell his vineyard to King Ahab. She used her influence, of evil and greed, over King Ahab, to have an innocent man murdered. Elijah was sent by God to rebuke King Ahab for his actions, and for a moment the king repented, however, he continued his evil ways.

The way queen Jezebel lived her life and used her influence was a disgrace, shameful, and evil. Her actions brought death to innocent people. She used her influence to manipulate, control, and lead her husband and the children of Israel into unrighteousness. In a sense, Jezebel had deceived herself into thinking that she was a god. Her actions exulted themselves against the knowledge of God which symbolizes Satan at work in her life.

The lesson we can learn from Jezebel's life is that when we let the devil be in control of us and our authority, it leads to a life of "kill, steal, and destroy" (John 10:10a). Jezebel let an evil spirit control her and the spirit arouse from worshipping Baal-a false god. Repeatedly she chose to do the wrong thing and influenced others to follow her bad example. Jezebel's actions had severe consequences at the end of her life. The way she died was God's judgment (2 Kings 9:36). Her actions also affected King Ahab's lineage because God ended their reign (1 Kings 21:28-29).

When God gives us influence and we chose to honor and worship Him, it brings life to others. Others will benefit from our obedience and worship to God, especially when we are in a leadership position. When we use our influence to lead others to worship God, it makes their lives better, not worse.

Queen Jezebel's influence birthed destruction and death. Let us choose the influence God has given us to bring forth life through his son Jesus Christ.

Questions

1. We currently live in a society that urges us to participate in evil. How can we use our influence to cause others to turn to righteousness?

   _____

   _____

2. Have you ever been attacked because you choose to worship God and not Satan? What was that experience like? How did you overcome it?

   _____

   _____

3. Jezebel was a queen, but she used her authority for the kingdom of darkness. We are daughters of the King. God has given us the influence of his Kingdom on earth. How can we as women of God display our Kingdom's influence in our communities?

   _____

   _____

4. Have you ever encountered a Jezebel spirit, a spirit of control and power? How did you respond to it?

   _____

   _____

5. Who is a woman of influence that helped bring you the Life through the way she lived her life?

_____

_____

Prayer

Father God thank you for giving us Kingdom influence on the earth. We want to represent your righteousness in the land by the way we live our lives. Forgive us for any time we have turned away from you to follow another. Forgive us for any wrong we have done to the innocent. Holy Spirit, lead and guide us into righteousness so that we can lead others to worship the True and Living God. In Jesus' name, Amen.

About the Authors

Pastor Sharon Williams

Sharon Williams is a pastor and has been in ministry for over 48 years. She and her husband Daniel are founders of Go to Nations, a missionary sending agency working in 106 countries. As an ordained minister, Sharon was a part of the Christ the Redeemer Church Executive staff for 20 years. In 2010, Sharon began Act 4 the Nations, a non-profit organization working on 5 continents to help women attain a better way of life by partnering with missionaries and Anti-Human Trafficking organizations. You can find out more about Pastor Sharon Williams at www.act4nations.com and sharon@act4nations.com.

Pastor Dr. Shana Wise

Dr. Shana Wise is the Pastor and CEO of Wise Choice Ministries (est. 2016), a non-profit church ministry. She is the founder of The Well Christian Women's Network (est. 2016). Shana is the author of women's devotional, Acts of Intercession, The Impact of Your Election, and co-author of the Basic Ministry Training Manual, which are all available on Amazon. She received a Doctor of Divinity degree in 2019 from St. Thomas Christian University. Her passion is to teach and preach the gospel of Jesus Christ, equip others to apply the Word to their lives, and demonstrate the Word through the power of the Holy Spirit. Shana is married to Ron Wise and is the mother of four children. You can contact Pastor Shana Wise at www.wisechoiceministriesinc.com and wisechoiceinc@gmail.com.